Self-Esteem

Self-improvement By Increasing Your Self-Esteem, A Guide To Gaining Confidence And Enhancing Your Happiness

(A Guide To CBT And Positive Psychology To Overcome Self-Doubt)

Claude Patrick

TABLE OF CONTENT

Introduction 1
Chapter 1: Gain Influence Through Personal Development.. 4
Chapter 2: Managing Other People............................. 10
Chapter 3: Several Behaviors That Undermine Self-Esteem 15
Chapter 4: Negative Consequences Of Diminished Self-Esteem 20
Chapter 5: Accept Your Identity 27
Chapter 6: Realizing The Inferiority Mentality........ 35
Chapter 7: Managing Bad Days 44
Chapter 8: The Foundations Of Self-Esteem 55
Chapter 9: How Living With Purpose Functions.... 68
Chapter 10: How To Become A Superb Person? 74
Chapter 11: How To Construct Self-Esteem 91
Chapter 12: Experiment With Fairness 105
Chapter 13: Uncertainty Regarding Males 113
Chapter 14: The Components Of Self-Esteem. 132

Introduction

Parenting an adolescent is difficult. But being a teenager is also difficult, which is why our children need a trusted adult to rely on, seek advice from, and share their lives - the good, the bad, and the ugly.

Being in the front row of our children's lives is preferable to being on the topmost bleacher. Teenagers Today

The common cultural perception of a female adolescent is that she is erratic and moody, continually arguing with her mother over her freedom to speak her mind and her fashion choices. However, we rarely consider the demands that society places on a young girl as she matures from a child to a woman. The pressure on young females to be the ideal girl on social media, which inadvertently causes them stress and anxiety, is added to the already impossible mountain of expectations.

The purpose of this book is to explore the psychology of adolescent behavior in an effort to better comprehend and empathize with adolescents.

This book offers a psychological and scientific comprehension of the adolescent period. However, it uses a simplified approach and language to facilitate comprehension. Each scenario is accompanied by examples that provide the reader with a clear understanding of the phase an adolescent female goes through and the impact of social media on that phase. Although this book focuses on the effects of social media on adolescent females, it is applicable to all genders in modern parlance. In addition to providing psychological insight, the book meticulously dissects the addictive layout of social media and explains how, if left unchecked, they can contribute to a state of addiction. The book explains the necessity of fostering self-esteem and self-efficacy in adolescents, who would otherwise be susceptible to peer pressure in the absence of such development. In addition, it provides techniques and exercises for boosting their self-esteem. It reveals the variety of assaults that could be carried out via social media, such as cyberbullying, hacking, stalking, and doxxing. In addition, it explains why deprivation is not the solution and how the issue of social media addiction can be addressed in other ways. The concluding chapters focus on mental disorders and their consequences, such as suicidal tendencies.

This is required reading for all parents who wish to comprehend their adolescents better.

Chapter 1: Gain Influence Through Personal Development.

It is the natural privilege of every human being to be happy and free from life's sufferings. As normal as the geography and the seasons, happiness is the standard condition. Suffering is unnatural, and it is only due to our ignorance that we endure it. Wisdom is the source of happiness. To attain perfect wisdom, to fully comprehend the purpose of life, and to fully comprehend the relationship between mortal beings is to put an end to all suffering and to escape every ailment and evil that plagues us. Perfect wisdom is pure happiness.

Why do we endure in life? Because, in the grand scheme of things, we are being propelled forward in the evolution, we require the spiritual illumination that alone can illuminate the path and enable us to navigate the obstacles securely. Generally, we do not see or suspect the presence of trouble until it abruptly leaps out of the shadows like a barracuda. One day, our family unit will be complete and content. In the past week, death has passed and misery has supplanted happiness. When we acquire a companion. Why he will become an adversary in the future is unknown. Previously, we enjoyed wealth and all material comforts. There was an unanticipated change, and now we have nothing but poverty and distress, yet we search in vain for an explanation as to why this is the case. There was once a time when we had health and vitality, but they have both vanished with no apparent cause. Away from these minor catastrophes of life, numerous effects of lower consequence continue to bring us minor misery and suffering. We desperately wish to avoid them, but we cannot see them until they strike us, at which point, in our ignorance, we stumble upon them. The thing we guarantee is the spiritual illumination that will allow us to see far and wide, revealing the system by which the causes of mortal suffering can be avoided, and if we can only attain illumination, the evolutionary journey will be both comfortable and swift. It is as if we must traverse a lengthy, dark room with cabinetry haphazardly dispersed throughout. In the darkness, our movement would be sluggish and excruciating, and we would sustain numerous wounds. However, if we could press a button to activate the electric light, we could make the same journey swiftly and in complete safety and comfort.

The old system of education consisted of filling the mind with as much data, or purported data, as possible and polishing the individual's exterior. When a man is born, he is a complete finite being, and all that can be done for him is to load him up with information that he will use with greater or lesser skill, depending on his native capability. The theosophical concept is that the physical man, and all that constitutes his life in the physical world, is but a veritably partial expression of the Self; that in the pride of each there is virtually unlimited power and wisdom; that these can be expressed in the physical world as the physical body and its unnoticeable counterparts, which together constitute the complex vehicle of the pride's incarnation, are evolved and adapted to the purpose; an incarnation of the Self. Consequently, the light that leads to pleasure is extinguished from within, and the evolutionary journey that we are all on may be robbed of its misery.

Why does death cause suffering? Because it primarily separates us from those we adore. The only other reason why death causes grief or dread is because we do not comprehend it and its role in mortal evolution. The instant our ignorance is replaced by appreciation, however, similar anxieties vanish and are replaced by a calm contentment.

Why do we have adversaries whose words or actions cause us pain? Due to the fact that our limited physical knowledge prevents us from perceiving the interconnectedness of all life and realizing that our erroneous thinking and actions must return upon us through others, a situation from which we can only escape by ceasing to believe wrong and patiently awaiting the time when the causes we've previously generated are exhausted. When spiritual illumination arrives, and we no longer stumble in the darkness of ignorance, the final foe will dissipate, and we will never again advance.

Why do individuals experience poverty and discontent? Only because of our bumbling ignorance, which makes their existence possible for us, and because we do not fathom their meaning and assignments nor know the appropriate stance to take toward them, do they exist. We would no longer be troubled by them if we had the intelligence to comprehend why they occur to individuals and why they are essential to their development. When nature's task is fully mastered, these silent preceptors will vanish.

Similarly, we observe all forms of suffering. They are responses from our naïve blunders and preceptors that indicate the best course of action. When we have mastered the assignments, we are informed that they are no longer necessary and they vanish. Men do not become wise and renowned through the acquisition of external data. It is by cultivating the soul from within until it floods the intellect with the brilliant light of genius.

Chapter 2: Managing Other People

In all operations of persuasion, it is imperative to keep in mind that the most important factor is always and foremost an agreeable sensation in the minds of the target audience. You should not attempt to persuade a person to act in your favor until he has developed a favorable opinion of you. This is the original highest stair. Once such a condition has been met, you are also prepared for the flamboyant assault.

When dealing with other people and attempting to magnetically persuade them to do what you want, you should conjure the general glamorous sensation within yourself, will them to do as you request, and simultaneously consider them to be previously subscribing and acting. Your inner state should be impeccably calm, buoyant, and optimistic, regardless of the external means employed. Your mind should be focused on the object requested, and its success should be regarded as already assured. The person's response may be delayed, but you shouldn't be discouraged because some minds don't accept suggestions (those pertaining to your inferred will) immediately, nor do they act rashly in response to their research. It's always in style to convince people that they're acting on their own whim or judgment; they should be made to feel utterly liberated, unrestrained, and that they're doing their own will instead of yours because they want to.

All of these ideas can be summed up in the words of a distinguished scientist: "Life is not a braggart who struts out into the open macrocosm, disrupting the laws of energy in all directions, but rather a master strategist who, seated in his secret chamber over his cables, directs the movements of a vast army." This is an excellent definition of enchantment.

The success-engagement hypothesis We are now prepared to discuss the application of the grand supposition principle of captivation.

Consider everything as previously attained and every endeavor as previously accomplished.

Importance of Self-Esteem

Self-esteem is our perception of ourselves. When conditions are favorable, we have confidence and self-respect. We are pleased with who we are, what we can accomplish, and our level of competence. Despite the fact that it can fluctuate, self-esteem is primarily stable and consistent. A healthy sense of self-worth encourages perseverance and optimism in life.

Self-esteem affects not only our beliefs, but also our emotions and behaviors. It has significant effects on our satisfaction and life quality. It has a significant effect on our relationships, careers, aspirations, and how we care for ourselves and our offspring.

Although difficult circumstances such as breakups, illness, or loss of income may temporarily lower our self-esteem, we rapidly recover to think positively about ourselves and the future. Even when we fail, our sense of self-worth remains unaffected. Those with healthy self-esteem give themselves credit when things go well, and when they don't, they look beyond themselves and objectively evaluate their faults and mistakes. They then improve them.

Self-respect is not solely dependent on a single product or mindset. Rather, a person's perception of all the characteristics that make up who they are as a person, such as their personality, successes, talents, and abilities, as well as their history, will determine how they are perceived.

Their self-esteem is comprised of experiences, relationships, and physical appearance.

When constructing their self-image and determining how they feel about themselves, each individual may place a greater emphasis on certain factors that affect their self-esteem, such as their appearance, relationship status, abilities, or professional accomplishments (or lack thereof).

Chapter 3: Several Behaviors That Undermine Self-Esteem

Comparison

When comparing ourselves to others, we frequently place more emphasis on our differences than on our similarities. This type of comparison can perpetuate the feeling that our fundamental requirements and desires are unfulfilled.

Instead of focusing on the future, clinging to the past causes one form of self-comparison. Perhaps you were in better shape ten years ago. You were previously married but are now unmarried.

Even though we frequently romanticize the past, nostalgia is easy to experience. Because we cannot return to the past

When we look back, we discover that we are never contented with the present.

Self-esteem and self-comparison go hand in hand without a doubt. Test your own self-evaluations. Confront the inner voice that continually tells you you are inadequate. If you recognize that self-comparison plays a role in your life, you can learn to manage your internal reactions and expectations.

Internalizing Unfavorable Feelings

Children are the first to teach others how to gain what they want or need by pleasing their mothers. As children become adults, they may fail to win over their colleagues, resulting in negative outcomes.

criticism. Because of what they have done or who they are, certain individuals choose to internalize their detrimental behaviors. Keeping these beliefs lowers one's sense of worth and self-esteem directly. An ongoing loss of self-esteem or a sense of unworthiness causes anxiety and depression, which worsen if these negative emotions are not replaced with new opportunities to experience life's validation.

Dieting

Dieting is indicative of a poor body image and diminished self-esteem. Every time you deviate from your diet, you experience negative emotions that you carry with you, causing you to be self-conscious and anxious about what others will think.

folks consider you. By imposing unachievable and hazardous dietary restrictions on yourself, you often set yourself up for failure. Although weight loss is a common side effect of consuming healthier foods, this is not the intended result. Dieting for the sole purpose of weight loss and failing to achieve this goal is devastating.

Having unfavorable friends

People who ridicule you for not acting appropriately or not being "thin enough" may have a negative effect on your self-esteem. You probably already hold yourself responsible for the same things. Having such beliefs frequently validated by peers is sufficient to convince one that they are true. It is time to act.

a few new, upbeat friends if this is the case.

Constantly Being Positive

Although optimism is generally beneficial, there are times when it can be detrimental. When it comes to anything that could potentially injure you in the short or long term, making the best of a bad situation is not always the best course of action. Receiving a mediocre grade in class or a poor evaluation at work are both things you can and must improve. Your self-esteem and self-worth may suffer if you accept a negative grade or evaluation with the attitude, "Oh well, it's just once."

Ask questions instead. Determine the solutions, then proceed with action. Your

The likelihood of receiving higher grades or performing better on the job is likely to increase, and you can't get enough of that. Regularly receiving positive feedback, especially when it is the result of your own efforts, can improve low self-esteem more than you might expect.

Chapter 4: Negative Consequences Of Diminished Self-Esteem

Your self-image is likely to develop and change as you age, go through life, and respond to significant life events, just like everything else.

People tend to have a fixed level of self-esteem, whether it is high, low, or somewhere in the middle. A poor self-image influences every aspect of life, including social interactions, attentiveness, emotional control, decision-making, and life satisfaction.

Reactivity

When you have high self-esteem, it is simpler for you to recover from negative situations and opinions.

or attitudes that others may have toward you. Conversely, if you have a low self-concept, you are more likely to take rejection or criticism personally and to assume that other people's problems are all your fault.

As a consequence of this combination, people with low self-esteem may become more sensitive to everyday events and interpersonal interactions. Low self-esteem makes it more difficult for individuals to manage their emotions, overcome obstacles, and maintain a positive outlook on life.

Low self-esteem frequently causes small problems to develop into larger, seemingly insurmountable issues, thereby lowering one's self-esteem.

Moodiness

Low self-esteem is more complex than simply being miserable or having a bad day. Everyone experiences unhappiness when bad things occur, but these feelings typically pass and, particularly for those with high self-esteem, do not significantly affect one's sense of self-worth. In contrast, low self-esteem is a persistently negative self-image that, although it may fluctuate in response to positive and negative events, persists over time regardless of your current circumstances.

Your level of self-esteem may be influenced by upbringing, colleagues, and life events, as well as genetics, personality types, and other factors. However, as stated previously, when self-esteem is extremely low, it

may place you at risk for numerous mental health problems.

Prone to Depression

The correlation between mental health issues and low self-esteem is especially strong. Contrary to conventional belief, research demonstrates conclusively that low self-esteem causes depression, not vice versa. Therefore, melancholy does not result in a low self-esteem. Rather, a negative self-image increases the likelihood of developing depression.

In addition, research indicates that a stronger sense of self protects against mental health issues, possibly as a result of better coping mechanisms, greater optimism, and a more positive outlook on life.

The resilience that results from this more receptive and affirming internal dialogue. When you have low self-esteem, you feel bad about yourself, which makes it more challenging to live a full life, achieve your goals, and maintain healthy interpersonal and romantic relationships.

Critically, research indicates that low self-esteem is strongly linked to suicidal ideation, eating disorders, substance misuse, emotional issues, despair, and anxiety. According to research, low self-esteem is also significantly associated with anxiety disorders, particularly social phobias and social anxiety disorder.

Risky Behavior

In addition, research links low self-esteem to an increased likelihood of engaging in unhealthy behaviors, notably during adolescence, such as drug and alcohol abuse, driving under the influence, self-harm, smoking, and carrying a weapon.

In essence, those who esteem and respect themselves the least are more likely to make decisions that put their health and wellbeing at risk.

In addition, it has been demonstrated that increasing one's self-esteem may aid in the rehabilitation of substance abuse. This link between low self-esteem and poor decision-making appears to be especially pronounced in adolescents, whose still-developing executive function abilities place them at a disadvantage when making choices.

Low Self-Assurance

In addition, high self-confidence fosters self-reliance, self-advocacy, and faith in oneself and one's talents, all of which contribute to high self-esteem and serve as a foundation for outstanding mental health and quality of life.

Chapter 5: Accept Your Identity

A lack of self-acceptance may hinder you in all facets of your existence. It undermines your self-assurance and may prevent you from reaching your maximum potential.

Individuals with a high level of self-acceptance are more resistant to criticism. They acknowledge that it is acceptable to accept oneself while concurrently pursuing continuous self-improvement. What, however, is self-acceptance? And why are some people more tolerant of themselves than others? How does it benefit you, and what can you do to cultivate it? Let's find out. Self-acceptance is the process of accepting oneself and all of one's personality traits as they are. You embrace them regardless of whether they are positive or negative. This includes both your physical and mental characteristics. Self-acceptance involves recognizing that your value transcends your particular characteristics and actions.

This is occasionally referred to as radical self-acceptance. Self-acceptance provides greater self-assurance and makes one less receptive to criticism. It means to accept each and every aspect of oneself unconditionally and without exception. To achieve self-acceptance, you must learn to embrace the undesirable or repulsive aspects of yourself. This is why so many of us struggle to accept ourselves. We prefer to conceal, ignore, and deny the parts of ourselves that we deem undesirable. We prefer to modify them rather than embrace them. Self-acceptance does not merely entail embracing our undesirable traits and giving up on attempting to change them. On the contrary, it implies that we are aware of our faults but have no emotional attachment to them. This self-awareness may assist us in modifying our behavior and forming healthier practices. A dearth of self-acceptance limits one's capacity for enjoyment. Additionally, it affects your mental and emotional health. It keeps you focused on your worst qualities, and these negative thoughts produce unpleasant emotions. Self-acceptance may provide you with more self-assurance. It assists you in understanding that your perceived undesirable characteristics do not characterize you or your worth.

Despite your anxieties, you are more likely to act when you have confidence. In contrast, a lack of self-acceptance may hinder you and prevent you from pursuing your goals. Self-acceptance enables you to recognize that failure does not define you and is always an opportunity for growth along the path to success. Additionally, confidence may grant you more latitude. It assists you in making decisions without soliciting the approval of others. When you lack self-acceptance, you are constantly attempting to conceal, repress, and suppress your true nature. This may cause you to feel exhausted. Some individuals are naturally more tolerant of themselves than others. Have you ever pondered the reason for this? Because our early experiences influence the degree to which we embrace ourselves as adults. Our parents or caregivers are the first to inform us which of our characteristics are acceptable and which are unacceptable. As children, we learn to embrace only those aspects of ourselves that others accept. We view the other aspects of ourselves as flawed, and we reject, deny, and attempt to hide them. The difficulty, however, is that these evaluations are arbitrary. They rely on your parents' or caregivers' values and priorities. For instance, numerous emotions are considered acceptable in different households. If you were raised in a home where anger was unacceptable, you may be unable to accept the parts of yourself that experience anger or rage. Your levels of self-acceptance are also affected by parenting style. Children accept as fact each and every criticism their parents cast at them. Consequently, if your parents were extremely critical or demanding, the voice of your inner critic will likely be strong, and you may also have a dread of failure.

On the other hand, individuals with more compassionate parents tend to exhibit greater self-compassion.

Children also lack the ability to differentiate between their behavior and themselves. They believe that if their behavior is objectionable, it follows that they are also undesirable.

Therefore, children of critical parents are more likely to struggle with self-acceptance. People with greater levels of self-acceptance are more likely to have parents who were more positive and encouraging. You now understand why self-acceptance is essential. However, do not take our word for it.

I have compiled some of the most uplifting self-acceptance quotes from some of our beloved philosophers. Save these and refer to them whenever you need a little encouragement on the path to self-acceptance.

Because genuine belonging is only possible when we present our actual, defective selves to the world, our sense of belonging will never exceed our level of self-acceptance. Brené Brown, academic

"You can search the entire world for someone more deserving of your affection and devotion than yourself, but such a person does not exist anywhere. You, more than anyone else on the planet, are deserving of your love and affection." — Sharon Salzberg, author

"Because one has self-confidence, one does not attempt to persuade others. Because one is satisfied with oneself, one does not need the approbation of others. Because one embraces himself or herself, the entire universe embraces him or her." — Lao Tzu, philosopher

"I do not know if I will continue to be the same person even now. However, I've learned over the years to absolve myself. Anyone who lives will make mistakes; this is inevitable. But once you do and perceive the mistake, you forgive yourself and say, "Well, if I had known better, I would have done better." Maya Angelou was a poet and activist.

Self-acceptance may facilitate self-compassion, even when things go awry. It can assist you in maintaining a balanced and objective perspective of yourself. Self-acceptance will provide you with happiness and fulfillment independent of external factors.

Chapter 6: Realizing The Inferiority Mentality

No person is perfect. Each individual is defective and deficient in ways that make him feel inferior when compared to others. A man may be extraordinarily intelligent and accomplished, but harbor profound insecurities. While he may appear confident on the surface, he is actually plagued with inadequacy. He always assumes that new acquaintances will dislike him. When he allows these feelings of inadequacy and inferiority to permeate every aspect of his being, his natural functioning is impaired. A dearth of self-esteem is known as an inferiority complex. It is a feeling that causes self-doubt and casts doubt on your capacity to achieve something. It is a condition that causes you to withdraw or act aggressively out of embarrassment. You believe that you do not live up to the expectations of others. Unchecked, it can destroy your existence. It causes you to agonize internally due to emotional conflicts, which can lead to harmful mental states. When you have an inferiority complex, you may feel unworthy compared to others. Your social status, physical defects, or mental deficiency may be to blame. Because you are dissatisfied with your own characteristics, you wish you were someone else: someone who is more confident, more attractive, or more talented. You disregard the fact that you were endowed with specific physical, emotional, and cognitive abilities for your vital life mission. According to psychiatrists, inferiority complexes may have real or imagined causes. It stems from your own beliefs. Your emotions are affected by the inferiority complex you've created in your mind. You behave as if you are that person because you believe you are that person. Typically, inferiority complexes emerge during infancy. When you are young, you may be weaker than other children, making you the target of abuse and teasing. You are given labels such as "dumb," "weak," "awkward," and "clumsy," among others. When you allow your mind to embrace these labels as true, you become a victim of inferiority complex. If it is not processed or discarded during your formative years, it will have an effect on your adult existence. During adolescence, you are more susceptible to this sensation because you are developing your own identity. During this time, you are beginning to increase your self-esteem by receiving compliments for your accomplishments. You are acquiring new knowledge and confidence-boosting experiences as you acquire new skills.

You have the opportunity and freedom to experience life. However, it is also the most crucial period, as your childhood experiences will either drive or pull you away from the actions necessary for maturing and developing your personality. It will remain with you until you attain adulthood. Even as an adult, you can experience inferiority complexes, especially when you feel incapable of achieving an objective you are pursuing. When you feel that you are far from realizing your ambition and that the odds are not in your favor, you become depressed and frustrated. In addition, your mind replays instances of inadequacy when you experience these negative emotions. You believe you lack the necessary skills to complete the assignment because you anticipate failing again. When those closest to you treat you as a member of a lower social class, repressed feelings of distress and sorrow surface. You realize that your childhood memories continue to hold you captive.

Who are the victims of inferiority complex?

People who are raised in a negative environment often struggle with inferiority complex. They were reared in a home where criticism was prevalent. When children fail to meet their parents' standards, they are made to feel inadequate, judged by others, ridiculed, and humiliated.

As infants, those who constantly seek affirmation from others or attention for themselves are frequently victims of an inferiority complex. They lack self-confidence and rely on the support of others to boost their spirits. Due to their struggles with anxiety and melancholy when alone, they require social interaction. They may engage in bullying to gain attention or to conceal their own feelings of inadequacy. Their aggression is a mask for their own insecurities.

Additionally, individuals with inferiority complexes are more likely to have been spoiled as infants. They become reliant on those around them and expect them to fulfill their needs. They consistently seek assistance from others, particularly during difficult times.

Those belonging to minority organizations. When they feel inferior to or discriminated against by the majority, they frequently conceal physically and figuratively in order to avoid being humiliated. They feel inferior, so when they are made fun of, they become agitated but attempt to conceal their emotions. If the sentiments are not addressed by an adult or someone in a position of authority, they will affect the individual's outlook and way of life.

People born into low-income families may also erroneously construe their situation as justification for inferiority complexes. When they believe they are the target of discrimination based on social status, they become enraged and have a tendency to isolate themselves from others. They develop aberrant behavior and become increasingly frustrated with their life circumstances.

Because you believe that everything negative that happens to you is your fault, inferiority complex impairs your cognitive functioning and causes you to make errors. Your rationality may be impaired. Occasionally, you make decisions that you later come to repent. Low motivation and anxiety are the consequences. Stressors amplify and impede your capacity to perform the task effectively. A frightening disease is not inferiority complex. Because of this disease, your mind begins to believe that you do not merit the best things in life. It is only a negative concept if you believe you do not deserve it. However, if you know how to convert this emotion into motivation to accomplish more in life, it can also be your ticket to success. Use this emotion to increase your vitality and focus your attention so that you can improve yourself. As a result, you may become more motivated to improve your situation and work harder to attain success. As a result, you may be more productive and enjoy life more. It is a very powerful propelling force. Do not let little setbacks undermine your confidence. Changing your perspective is the key to success.

Is inferiority complex regarded as a mental disorder?

The individual with an inferiority complex has low self-esteem, which is a psychological condition and not a disorder. Negative experiences, past traumas, and formative comparisons are some of the causes of feelings of inferiority. It can exacerbate anxiety and other mental health conditions if not handled appropriately. There are two distinct inferiority complexes.

Fundamental inferiority complex: This often occurs when children are held to a higher standard than their peers in both academic and extracurricular activities. Later on, the same child is affected by these occurrences.

Secondary inferiority complex: This develops as an adult as a consequence of childhood experiences. The individual may have trouble performing simple duties.

Chapter 7: Managing Bad Days

There will be instances in which your child is injured despite your best efforts to secure them. Then, there will simply be bad days; as any parent of a preschooler can attest, bad days are inevitable. Parents can play a crucial role in teaching their children how to manage with these difficult circumstances.

Let's look at some strategies you can use to help your child through a difficult day.

Listening attentively is the initial step. Permit your child to characterize the problem without interfering or adding your own interpretation. Even if they allow their children to respond, parents should refrain from asking inquiries in a demanding manner.

2. Allow your child to vent, then demonstrate that you share her concerns by echoing what she said. In response to your child's statement, "Everyone laughed at me when I didn't know the answer," you can say, "I realize it must have been horrible when the other children laughed."

3. Validate your child's feelings. Some parents, including myself, are prone to respond, "I'm sure it was nothing" or "You're making too much of it," in an attempt to "play down" the insult. Such comments may encourage your child to respond more vehemently the next time he argues his point.

A parent may inquire, "What did you do to cause him to say that?" in an effort to comprehend what transpired. Instead, avoid making judgmental remarks like these. Accusing your child will prevent you from communicating with him or her.

5. Prepare for an improved day tomorrow. Discuss a creative way for your child to ask the instructor for help or devise a response to teasing that your child can use. Before you send your child to school the next day, remind her of the conversation.

A change in routine can occasionally distract a child from negative emotions and demonstrate that you are there to assist him. A mother takes her son out for frozen yogurt and some one-on-one time when he appears distressed.

7. To help your child feel rejuvenated and ready for the next day, you can also try putting him or her to bed earlier after a stressful day.

Physical Affection: Exhibit physical affection when required. Even though you shouldn't force your child to embrace or cuddle you, some children do benefit from physical contact at the end of a difficult day. Occasionally, all a baby needs to feel safe and cherished is a parent's embrace.

Make Them Feel secure: By listening to and empathizing with your child, you can help him or her feel secure when talking to you. Keeping to your routine will also reassure your infant. Try to maintain your normal routine instead of allowing a bad day to undermine everything. Children perceive routine as secure because it fosters a sense of anticipation. Lastly, reassure your children that they can depend on you and that your home is safe.

Give Your Child Space: After you have checked in, you may need to give your child space. Some children require alone time following a trying day. Some individuals simply require a bite and a nap. You are the expert on your child, so if you feel that the time is not right for a prolonged discussion, take a step back and give your child space.

11. Create a memorable occasion with your family by preparing something tasty, such as banana bread, brownies, or cookies. Permit your child to perform the majority of the task (and decorating). Take numerous photographs! This will improve one's disposition (particularly when it's time to sample the final product).

12. Assemble a riddle. Puzzles are soothing activities that encourage conversation and relaxation.

Investigate the library. Children's dispositions are always enhanced by perusing the book aisles and making a purchase to take home. On the journey home, they will enjoy relaxing in the car and reading their books.

Be proactive. Set up an obstacle course in your living room, throw a dance party, or have a water balloon battle. Physical activity enhances not only your children's disposition, but also their academic performance and sleep quality.

15 Perform some music. The proper music can improve our concentration, increase our stamina, and distract us from pain and fatigue. The right music can dramatically alter your mindset.

Get inside the vehicle. Occasionally, a leisurely city tour is exactly what everyone requires. Simply navigate the city while wearing a seatbelt and listening to music. You may choose to make a quick stop at the drive-through for an ice cream treat, or you may choose to drive through your beloved city or rural areas. Everyone receives some quiet, reflective time as a result.

Colorize the content. Bring out the pastels, colored pencils, and coloring books. Coloring is soothing and relaxing while listening to music or an audiobook.

18. Say "thank you." Create a gratitude receptacle or other daily gratitude practice. Have your child place a thank-you note in the receptacle at the close of each day. As a consequence, he may be able to default to optimism. (The entire family will enjoy this!)

Please embrace me. Hugs are the finest form of treatment. Children should be reminded of their ability to alter their emotions. However, when children are distressed, it may be challenging for them to recall the joyful and positive aspects of their lives. You should remind them of the things that frequently enhance their mood at this time. I've observed that when you're feeling down, you appreciate drawing pictures of your favorite characters or listening to your favorite music. You can help your children recover from a difficult day and develop problem-solving skills by providing them with this simple reminder.

Here are some catchphrases that you can use to cheer up your children (of any age) on a poor day.

I adore you.

Would you like a hug?

Do you desire to talk about it?

I'm available to you.

It will all work out.

Is there any way I can assist?

I already idolize you.

Without a doubt, you will be able to resolve this situation.

Are you interested in ice cream?

You can count on us to calm your nerves.

Everyone experiences bad days, and it is permissible to experience such feelings.

Let's take a promenade and appreciate something beautiful.

You are intelligent, physically healthy, and attractive.

Never quit up! I am extraordinarily proud of you.

Deeply inhale and exhale your negative emotions.

You are not defined by your score on this exam.

I admire you and empathize with your predicament.

Remember that today is only one day in your entire existence.

Let's discuss it. It will elevate your spirits.

Let's engage in a pleasurable activity to increase our contentment.

Because I adore you, we will overcome this together.

Things will improve dramatically tomorrow.

I care about you and will back you in this endeavor.

Chapter 8: The Foundations Of Self-Esteem

Ten steps to constructing your self-esteem! "Five hints to acquire certainty!" How many self-help instructors have you heard make such rambling claims? Most likely many. However, if you had the opportunity to define self-esteem, how would you? Self-respect is the invulnerable arrangement of knowledge; it provides fortitude, resistance, and the ability to recover. Similar to our invulnerable constitution, self-esteem is innate, and we need it to face life's challenges. Calcium is a more appropriate association with self-esteem. Calcium strengthens our teeth and bones and is essential for a healthy body, whereas self-esteem is essential for a healthy mental disposition. While a calcium deficiency wouldn't necessarily result in death, our capacity to live a full life would be severely restricted. The same applies to self-esteem: We can survive without it, but we cannot live a complete life without it. Why is that the case? It has everything to do with how our self-esteem functions, which involves making specific assumptions about what we are willing to do. These assumptions influence our behavior to the extent that they transform it into the real world. Self-respect becomes a self-satisfying foresight. Consider the story of an alcoholic in recovery from the author's psychotherapy practice. He was about to secure the largest commission of his career as a draftsman, but instead of feeling energized, he was extremely restless and felt he did not deserve it. Why? As a consequence of his low self-esteem and low expectations for himself, he was unsuccessful. To calm his anxieties, he decided to drink, became extremely drunk, acted irresponsibly, and ultimately lost his job. Tragically, his low self-esteem was the cause of his demise. Given the importance of self-esteem to our knowledge, it is worthwhile to delve a bit deeper into the topic, commencing with the foundational beliefs upon which it is based. Self-respect genuinely boils down to something quite simple: we all reserve the right to be satisfied. This implies that people with high self-esteem will assert this privilege and do whatever is necessary to achieve it. Then again, we have low self-esteem when we permit our right to gratification to be subordinated.

How about we investigate this difference in detail? Consider the client who asked the author why she generally consented to married individuals who could not have cared less about her. This example began to make sense after the client disclosed that her father abandoned the family when she was a child, and her mother accused her. How does this relate to self-esteem? Her father's departure and her mother's hostility shaped her self-esteem by making her feel unworthy of affection. She eventually began to act in a manner that caused her existence to conform to this conviction. By yielding to married men who had repeatedly abandoned her, she supported the notion that she was without a doubt unworthy of affection. Low self-esteem manifests itself frequently in the following way: we decide on decisions that make our negative beliefs about others a reality, thereby harming ourselves in the process. Conversely, if we have high self-esteem, we are not only less likely to create problems for ourselves, but we are also better at persevering despite obstacles. Clinicians demonstrated this by assigning subjects with varying levels of self-esteem to the same task. Unbeknownst to the members, the projects contain several intractable problems. In any case, members with high self-esteem persist more than those with low self-esteem. This study demonstrates that our self-perception decisively determines how we respond to challenges; this is the power of self-esteem. Read on to determine how to approach it!

The mentality and behavior of living deliberately.

Therefore, how would we need to manufacture self-esteem? In general, it is not as theoretical as one might expect. It begins contemplating a rotating set. If we have any intention of working on our self-esteem, we must first begin living on purpose. Living intentionally does not entail a harmonious, exclusive method of coping with life of some kind or another. Living intentionally requires a willingness to recognize three discernment characteristics: realities, understanding, and emotion. Here is an essential example of how these three can become entangled: You feel wounded because you deduce from your partner's frowning that he is angry. Imagine a circumstance in which you did not observe him grimacing. If you realize that you may have misinterpreted his appearance, you can reevaluate your translations in a positive manner without responding internally. This mindset can be maintained by asking ourselves simple questions throughout the day, such as "How am I feeling right now?" "Why am I feeling this way?" and "Do my actions correspond to my emotions?" Thus, we will maintain contact with our inner universe. However, living intentionally is not just a mindset; it also requires instruction. We must continue to gather information from our current circumstances and adapt our actions accordingly. Here is a straightforward illustration of mindful living as a mindset and practice. Assume that you may wish to purchase another attire. You will have sorted this out by deliberately captivating your "interior world" or your desire to appear distinctive. However, you must also consider your external environment, or, more specifically, your financial situation - the "practice" aspect of your purchase. As this interaction takes into account both your feelings and your situation, you can rest assured that the decision you arrive at on your own is sensible. Living in this manner gives us a fundamental understanding of ourselves, which is essential for our prosperity.

2. Self-esteem will instruct you to recognize yourself and take responsibility for your own happiness.

Self-recognition, self-obligation, and self-respect. The initial two are so intertwined with the third that it is difficult to distinguish them; the fact that they share a similar prefix does not help! Regardless, the thing that matters is more obvious than you might expect. Self-recognition and self-responsibility are actions we take in order to increase our self-esteem in the future. When we decide to value ourselves, we practice self-recognition, which is the second pillar of self-esteem. For instance, have you recently committed an act that you regret? Have you ever spoken harshly to someone or ignored something you shouldn't have? Self-recognition does not imply that you endorse or approve of these negative behaviors; rather, it seeks to identify the underlying causes that led to them, such as feeling insulted or concerned about something else. If you comprehend why you reacted in this manner, you will be less likely to repeat this undesirable behavior. However, if we acknowledge our ongoing behavior, isn't there a risk that we'll become self-satisfied and lose motivation to change it? This is the dilemma: if you don't accept yourself as you are, you'll never find the motivation to progress because you'll spend all of your time focusing on your shortcomings. Self-recognition also continues to be closely associated with a sense of personal ownership. The obligation to oneself is the third pillar of self-esteem. It entails assuming control over your reality and your happiness through arrangement. This means posing the following question whenever an issue arises: "What can be done?" Instead of attempting to accuse others, take responsibility for your behavior. Instead of saying "He provokes me" or "I would act differently if, by some stroke of fate, she were to..." Remember that we must be satisfied by others. Indeed, this endeavor has a position for you! Recognizing this fact will help us engage with ourselves, a crucial aspect of self-esteem.

3. Self-esteem is self-determination; this requires defending yourself, which is surprisingly difficult.

"I reserve the privilege to exist" is a statement you can agree with, right? Presently, it is challenging for you to speak without reticence. In any case, doing this when you are alone feels somewhat demeaning. Whatever the case, why? The vast majority of us are unaware of this, and we frequently struggle to assert such a basic privilege. To include this, the creator questioned whether they accepted that they reserved the right to exist. Everyone agreed with the statement, but when asked to repeat it without hesitation, they hesitated and surprisingly sounded awkward. This unpretentious sense of trepidation regarding the declaration of our privileges is completely normal. It comes down to the following natural ways of thinking: "If I communicate my thoughts, I may provoke discontent," or "If I certify myself, I may provoke contempt." This mindset is an immediate barrier to developing our confidence, but we can overcome it by adhering to the fourth pillar of self-esteem: self-emphatics. Being self-confident is simply being one's true self. In addition, to practice self-emphatics, you must believe that your convictions are significant. For example, if you are at a party and you hear a hostile ethnic slur, you could say so. Daring to articulate one's opinion is a form of self-decision practice. Alternatively, you may have recently watched a film with your friends and been profoundly moved by it. Say so, and don't shrug apathetically out of a paranoid dread of being perceived as boring. Each time you express your ideas or advocate for your qualities, you strengthen your healthy self-esteem. Nevertheless, there are still two additional points of support for healthy self-esteem.

4. living purposefully and practicing individual reliability.

How would you like your existence to continue? Many would concur with the statement "with logic and dependability." These two qualities are, coincidentally, additional crucial pillars of self-confidence. As we build our confidence, it is essential that we first feel ownership over our objectives. By asking yourself what you need and where you need to go, you have begun to proactively use the fifth pillar of self-esteem, living intentionally, to your advantage. In any case, this is demonstrably not the case. You must continue monitoring your progress. This can be seen in Jack's narrative. Jack had a lifelong aspiration to become an essayist, but instead of honing his skills, he chose to merely observe.

Chapter 9: How Living With Purpose Functions

"The purpose of existence is not happiness. It is to be helpful, to be respected, to be empathetic, and to have your life make a difference that you have lived well." The philosopher Ralph Waldo Emerson

Have you reached the point where perplexity, yearnings, emptiness, melancholy, and the sensation of something missing converge? And it's even worse when they manifest when you feel as though the weight of the universe is on your shoulders.

The simplest duties, such as getting out of bed each morning, become burdensome, and the greatest pleasures of life, such as making new friends and spending time with family, become unsatisfying. Things appear convoluted and severe to the point of intolerability.

However, before you get back on your feet, you must realize that your life can still be altered by learning how to live with purpose.

In the first few chapters, you have learned the fundamentals of living on purpose, what you want your life to look like, and how to set and maintain your goals. In this chapter, you will understand how living with purpose actually functions.

Before anything else, one must be familiar with the various varieties. There is the so-called "macro" level and "micro" level when living a purposeful existence.

For micro-level purposes, this is when you become aware of all your values and begin to integrate them. Once you comprehend what it is

You stand for them, do what you believe in, and your sense of self-worth and confidence will increase, despite the fact that the situation could be terrible.

However, this is merely a minor aspect of living on purpose.

Regarding the macro level, this is a completely separate issue.

Here, this is the larger picture.

This is the time when you seek your purpose.

This is your ultimate goal.

This is when you wake up every morning knowing you are headed in the direction you desire, regardless of what others believe.

To understand how to live with purpose, you must discover the lacking piece of the puzzle. What exactly is this? It is the realization that your ultimate purpose is to give, not to receive.

Purpose - such as pleasure and success - is paradoxical at its core, despite the fact that everyone strives to improve themselves and their lives.

It would be advantageous if you never sought achievement, because the more you pursue it and make it your objective, the more likely you are to miss it.

Like pleasure, success is not something to be pursued. This must happen. If you want money, help others to make money! If you want people to adore you, you must first embrace them.

And once you've accomplished this, once you've been of service to others, everything falls into place, and you uncover who you truly are and what your life's true purpose is.

Chapter 10: How To Become A Superb Person?

1. Change

To better yourself, you must adapt.

Change is the best method to develop and advance as the person you must become. Many individuals are opposed to change, which can make growth extremely challenging.

When you maintain an open mind and are willing to change, you will improve your skills and grow into the person you need to be.

2. Quit Rationalizing

When I first began my organization in high school, I made excuses whenever something went wrong. I would censure others, including the client or any other person. Regardless, I could never hold myself accountable for negative outcomes.

Overall, I've learned that accepting responsibility for your mistakes is crucial. I stopped rationalizing, took responsibility when it was truly my error, and had the opportunity to accomplish much more. By recognizing that I had made a mistake, I was able to learn from my blunders, thereby contributing to my personal development.

3. Quit Being Furious

Many individuals allow anger and wrath to alter their cognitive abilities. Growing up, I was a passionate individual, but I observed that it harmed my relationships with others and increased my blood pressure.

Extremely difficult to master, but immensely advantageous, is the ability to control one's anger. Instead of lashing out, I decided to work out how to alter my pessimistic disposition. Keeping my anger does not assist me or solve any problems. It simply produces a larger quantity.

4. Set a positive example

Occasionally, you should serve as a model for others in order to better yourself. When I became a business visionary and people began to revere me, I became considerably more circumspect in my actions. I would have preferred not to discourage people by demonstrating my youth or being a role model.

You can start small by being a "older sibling" to someone, mentoring a children's group, or setting a positive example for your children. Always choose actions that your admirers will appreciate.

5. Pardon Somebody

Forgiving someone who has wronged you is unquestionably difficult. When I became enraged with someone for carrying out an action, I would never forgive them. Regardless of how trivial it was, I would hold it against them until the end of their existence, which was detrimental.

I quickly learned that humans are prone to making mistakes. Instead of holding someone's mistakes against them eternally, try to pardon them. To learn how to be a good person and happy, you must examine your past and forgive those who have caused you damage.

6. Concentrate on Individuals

People are busy with their occupations, families, and livelihoods. Everyone is in a haste, yet individuals rarely have the time or the will to listen to what others have to say. I've learned that listening to people and allowing everyone a voice is arguably the best thing you can do.

I was able to meet some of the most remarkable individuals, complete the most lucrative deals, and cultivate relationships that will last a lifetime because I took the time to listen to people.

7. Be trustworthy

Nowadays, it is difficult to discover attractive individuals. Nonetheless, authenticity is the optimal response in every circumstance. Guarantee yourself that you will not deceive for the next month.

By cultivating positive habits, you can challenge yourself to speak the truth. If you are a compulsive liar, start small by telling the truth for a single day. After achieving a more modest objective, raise it by 2 or 3 points. This may be the greatest piece of advice on how to become the person you want to be.

8. Perform a task you would rather avoid

Keeping an open mind and trying things you wouldn't normally do is a simple way to develop personally. Face a challenge and dare yourself to attempt something you've always been afraid to do. You will continue living your greatest life once you leave.

9. Stun Someone Extraordinary

Do you have any close friends, relatives, or cherished ones in your life? Whether it's your spouse/significant other, your children, or a relative, prepare a special delicacy for them. If you know someone who deserves a good vacation or other gift, buy it for them.

Possibly the most rewarding sensation on earth is realizing that you made someone smile. Amaze the extraordinary person in your life by performing something unusual for them!

10. Give Consideration to Your Own Needs

While you have no control over every situation you encounter, you can influence how you respond. Moreover, your future depends on how well you take care of yourself. When you confront yourself, you will grow as a person and be able to overcome the challenges of your current situation.

Taking care of oneself is essential for developing adaptability when confronting obstacles. When you are exhausted and consume unhealthy food throughout the day, you are likely to respond to the challenges you face in ordinary life. In the current situation, responding can create additional problems for you and others. For effective problem-solving, you must give careful consideration to your body, mind, and spirit.

You wish to: relax

Rest: Rest plays an important role in advancing your physical and domestic prosperity. Insufficiency of sleep weakens your immune system, impairs your ability to concentrate, and induces erratic behavior close to home. Sleep deprivation can have negative effects on the body. The average adult requires seven to nine hours of sleep per night to function optimally.

Consume a variety of nutrient-dense foods on a regular basis if you want to feel happy and vivacious. A poor eating pattern will consistently leave you feeling exhausted and bloated. Consistently consuming vegetables and organic foods will not only improve your health, but also help you maintain a positive outlook on life.

Routinely interacting with others is one of the most effective means of coping with problems and negative emotions. While attempting to create opportunities for friends and family or voicing your concerns, mingling will make you a better individual.

*Personal time: You should schedule adequate time for yourself. This requires setting aside time for contemplation, journaling, and reflection. Consistently engaging in these activities will unquestionably improve your ability to handle complex issues and your overall well-being.

Chapter 11 of the SE: Relationship

It could be your partner if you're struggling with confidence.

If you're in a relationship with someone who always despises you, you should evaluate whether it's worthwhile. In most instances, this is not the case. Even if you have children and choose to "continue for the sake of the children," you are not helping them. You are teaching them that it is acceptable for others to not respect them.

Respect is owed to all parties in a relationship. If you're not receiving it, this could be the cause of your lack of confidence.

You must carefully consider why you are in this relationship and what you hope to gain from it. I cannot conceive of many reasons why I would stay in an abusive relationship.

I cannot think of anything in particular. I'm sorry to say it, but people who remain in this type of relationship and use their children as an excuse are pitiful. They are instructing their offspring in improper conduct.

If you are in a relationship with a person with whom you have no children and you are frequently reprimanded, you must either seek counseling to determine the source of the problem or end the relationship. It's that easy. If you have children with this individual, you must attend family counseling. If you have been married to this person for a while, it is likely that he or she has caused you and your children significant damage, but it is never too late to correct this error. Or defend yourself.

Eleanor Roosevelt once stated, "Only you can feel inferior." Many individuals fault those with whom they have a relationship for their loss of confidence. The opposite is true. Mrs. Roosevelt was on the mark. Only you can undermine your own self-assurance. Never delegate this authority to others.

People who find themselves in abusive relationships typically lack confidence in themselves. Relationship is not merely a symptom of disease. However, when a person is released from a toxic relationship, their confidence is always restored.

Taking control of your life, particularly in the sphere of relationships, can be extremely challenging. Your family and clergy may be pressuring you to maintain the relationship. They may have excellent intentions, but they may not comprehend the actual issue. And the true issue is not your spouse but rather yourself. You are the one who can permit slander against you.

You are the one who can allow confidence to be undermined. You are the only person who can consent to your own destruction.

Is the abuser to blame? Yes, certainly. However, he or she is not your concern.

Your issue is your complete lack of self-confidence and why you permit it to persist. You must resist, discipline yourself, and end the maltreatment.

Can someone who is abusive obtain assistance? Yes. You can enroll in a variety of programs designed to help you overcome your aggression issues. It is highly probable that a person who is abusive also lacks confidence and has a substance abuse or alcoholism problem. And you should urge them to obtain assistance.

Are you expected to remain with them during their counseling? Definitely not. After completing the counseling successfully, you can then work together to repair your marriage.

In the interim, you must concentrate on your own issues, which is why you permit the violence to continue or have even chosen to be in a relationship with an abusive partner. Then, you must focus on developing your confidence. Then and only then can you engage in any form of relationship.

The majority of us feel a sense of duty toward those with whom we have a relationship. And it is acceptable to feel a bond with them. But not at our expense.

If you are in a toxic relationship in which the other person is physically or psychologically abusive, you must take charge of your life and the relationship and take action.

Whatever it takes, terminate the relationship and distance yourself from the other party. You cannot sacrifice your sense of self-worth for the sake of your marriage or offspring. Long-term, children are better off living in a shack with you as a role model and someone they can revere than in a palace with you serving as a doormat.

This is because your children learn more about your relationship than they already know. And if you model a corrupt, dysfunctional relationship for them, they will likely imitate you as adults.

Chapter 11: How To Construct Self-Esteem

Your sense of worth will affect every aspect of your existence. Your self-esteem influences your work, relationships, and even physical and mental health. But what influences your perception of your talents and abilities specifically? Your sense of self-worth may have increased or decreased depending on how you've been treated in the past and the evaluations you've made of your life and your decisions. Discover yourself. Before a conflict, the wisest commander obtains a comprehensive understanding of his opponent. Without understanding your opponent, you cannot vanquish him. When attempting to overcome a negative self-perception and replace it with self-confidence, your worst adversary is yourself.

1 Determine who you are.

Start paying heed to your thoughts. Start maintaining a journal about yourself, your self-perception, and an analysis of the causes of your negative thoughts. Then, take into account your strengths, areas of expertise, and personal preferences. Consider whether your restrictions are genuine or the only ones you've allowed to be imposed unnaturally. You will ultimately emerge from the depths of yourself with increased self-esteem.

You do have some control over how much you value yourself, which is excellent news. You can make simple, practical adjustments that will exercise your body and mind. One such transition involves making an effort to eliminate negative thinking and increase positive, uplifting thoughts about the person you are and can be.

2 Positive Mentality Determines factors

If you want to increase positive thinking in your daily life, you must first identify the people, locations, and things that promote negative thinking. It could be your bank account balance or a persistently negative colleague. Certain circumstances are out of your control, but you can control how you react and perceive them. To do so, you must first recognize what causes you to feel anxious or despondent.

3 Take notes

A constant discourse, or "self-talk," occurs in your mind throughout the day.

This inner dialogue generates judgments about you and other individuals based on your current environment. So allow yourself some time to begin identifying patterns in this conversation. Does the evidence corroborate this viewpoint? Or does it frequently err on the side of illogic, constantly assuming the worst?

4 Question your assumptions

If you observe yourself making assumptions or perpetually downplaying your positive qualities, you must intervene and inject some positive thinking into your self-talk. Learning to motivate oneself and think positively is comparable to building muscle. The ability to think positively, to forgive oneself for errors, and to learn to give oneself credit for accomplishments requires daily mental exercise. You should exert effort. Maybe you've always wanted to climb a mountain, spend the night in a tent, or go kayaking, but you've never had the chance. The more we push ourselves to attempt new things, the more we realize what we're truly capable of, which helps us develop self-confidence.

5 Compile an inventory.

If you're unsure of where you stand in terms of self-esteem, a personal attributes inventory can be useful. Indicative of your tendency to be overly critical of yourself is if you find yourself cataloguing more flaws than virtues. Consider the talents, passions, and interests that you do not currently list or have not yet identified. Never assume you know everything about yourself and your capabilities. Those with high self-esteem are encouraged to engage in daily self-discovery. Determine your values, then examine your life to determine where they are not being carried out. Afterwards, make any necessary modifications. The more you understand what you stand for, the more self-assured you will feel.

Recognize your accomplishments.

People with low self-esteem frequently attribute their successes to luck or coincidence. Or, instead of accentuating their progress, they may emphasize their shortcomings. People with high self-esteem make the effort to acknowledge their accomplishments. They respond to compliments with "Thank you," as opposed to dismissing them. Consequently, those with high self-esteem are not always conceited or narcissistic; rather, they have confidence in their abilities and acknowledge their achievements when they occur. Recognize the small victories.

You rose promptly this morning. Tick. Your eggs were poached to perfection. Winning. Celebrating small victories is an excellent way to develop confidence and begin to feel better about yourself. Consider all of your accomplishments, then write them down. Create an inventory of everything you've accomplished that you're pleased with, everything you've done well. Review your list when you need a reminder of your capacity to complete tasks successfully.

Celebrate your successes. Take the time to acknowledge your accomplishments, no matter how insignificant they may seem. It could also be beneficial to recall past successes.

Accept accolades. You could make a note of them to review whenever you feel down or have self-doubt.

Ask others what they appreciate about you. It is probable that they perceive you differently than you perceive yourself.

Do not place excessive importance on negatives. If someone says something unhelpful or unkind, you may find yourself concentrating on the negative and ignoring the positive.

Create a list of qualities you appreciate about yourself. For instance, you could include personality traits, skills or experience, beliefs or causes that are important to you, or activities that you enjoy. You could also solicit the opinions of others.

Understanding self-esteem, including its effects, your level of self-esteem, and what it entails.

Self-esteem is how we recognize and value ourselves. It is based on our perspectives and beliefs about ourselves, which can be difficult to alter at times. We could also refer to this as self-assurance.

Your self-esteem can influence whether you like and value yourself as a person, whether you can make decisions, defend yourself, whether you are willing to attempt new things and whether you recognize your strengths. It can also affect your self-compassion and your ability to move past your errors without unfairly blaming yourself.

Take the necessary time for yourself

Believe you have value and are adequate

Believe you deserve pleasure

Self-esteem, also known as self-worth and self-respect, is the degree to which an individual values himself. It can be modest or high. However, you should strive for a level of self-esteem that falls somewhere in the middle: healthy self-esteem.

Aspects Influencing Self-Esteem

Among the factors that can affect self-esteem are:

Age: Yes, your age can influence your self-esteem levels. This could be better exemplified by a situation in which you believe you are too young to do things for yourself.

Disability places a strain on your mental health and self-esteem because you are unable to perform certain tasks as normally abled people do. Normality, however, is subjective. You are able to define what is normal and what is not, as well as devise new ways to do things. Because you shine.

You are not popular or everyone's go-to person, and that is perfectly acceptable. But then, not being known by people at school or in the workplace could make you feel like you're not doing enough to be noticed. We've all been there, and it's a dreadful feeling, but you shouldn't allow it to define your capability. You are competent.

This occurs to everyone, at some point in their educational careers, when they believe they lack sufficient knowledge and are unable to contribute due to their lack of education.

Physical appearance; Physical characteristics such as hair, figure, height, weight, and skin color may also impact an individual's self-esteem.

Here, gender inequality comes into action. When men and women's liberties are not equal. But you recognize that we were not created equally.

Life experiences; traumatic experiences, the things from our past that partially define us. Not all life experiences are traumatic, but those that diminish our self-esteem are. It may be due to abuse, bereavement, or grief.

When you don't have enough money, many things go awry in your life, which you attribute to your lack of financial support. Yes, this does occur, and it contributes to your self-esteem. You do not believe you should be in a particular location because you do not have sufficient funds to mix with your 'rich' peers.

Implications of Self-Esteem

Self-esteem is indispensable. It improves physical well-being, self-awareness, mental well-being, healthy and satisfying interpersonal relationships, objectives, and overall well-being.

Similarly, low self-esteem can cause anxiety, depression, the inability to maintain healthy relationships, and failure.

Chapter 12: Experiment With Fairness

Have you ever pondered why there are those who have and those who do not? You may have been a little envious of those who are able to express themselves freely, as your lack of confidence prevents you from doing so. An Italian named Pareto conducted an experiment that led to the development of the 80/20 rule. 80 percent of the people in a particular region of Italy work very diligently, but only 20 percent reap the majority of the benefits. The most intriguing aspect of this premise is not its material application to the haves and have-nots. It applies to every aspect of existence as well. Many people miss out on the enjoyable portions of their lives because they do not know how to apply the rule to their situations. Allow me to demonstrate how this can boost your confidence.

Record your accomplishments in which you are confident

You may believe that this has little significance, but it does. You are adept at performing tasks within the household. You are self-reliant and regularly cleanse your teeth. You may be able to operate a car. What we require you to investigate are all of your areas of expertise. Now, we must consider the proportion of your life spent engaging in activities that make you feel uneasy and lack confidence. There are times when you perform tasks that do not make you feel joyful or fulfilled, but you do them anyway because that is what you do. Your self-esteem requires that you increase the proportion of time you spend doing things that make you feel good about yourself; consequently, you must spend more time doing things you are excellent at than doing things you are not.

Assume that you expend 20% of your time on activities that are detrimental to your self-esteem. Therefore, you should spend more time engaging in activities that make you feel like you have something positive to contribute to life. I would suggest that you devote more time to the activities listed below. Increase the amount of time you spend on activities that help you acquire self-confidence, and you will find that the amount of time you feel good about yourself will also increase. If you can increase that percentage daily and maintain a journal of what you did to increase it, you will find that your negative thoughts about yourself begin to fade away.

Reading and watching documentaries on television leads to education.

Crossword puzzles will increase your vocabulary.

Practicing mental games such as Luminosity – enhancing mental dexterity

Spending more time caring for yourself – thereby appreciating self-development

Spending more time with optimistic individuals helps you gain confidence.

Spending more time experimenting in the kitchen is extremely rewarding and can be shared with others.

Spending more time helping individuals you care about or those in need will always increase your positive self-perception.

In fact, when you realize that your approach to life affects what you receive from it, you realize that you have more control over your life than you may have initially believed. Additionally, this will enhance your confidence. You must advance in life, and it can be helpful to set small, daily objectives that you look forward to achieving. Make sure they are things that make you feel positive about who you are. Thus, the odds are in your favor, and you are able to enjoy life significantly more without continuously feeling inadequate. You do measure up, and you need to stop wasting time feeling miserable and incapable of expressing yourself. By selecting self-development activities, you are choosing to do something positive and thereby increasing your likelihood of experiencing happiness.

One thing I consistently neglected to do was take time for myself. Because everyone should have the same amount of time for self-improvement and life enjoyment, I now do this on a regular basis. When you write these numbers down and see them in black and white, you realize that 80% of your time is spent negatively and that you do not do enough to feel good about yourself. This is about figuring out who you are. Do not measure yourself by the opinions of others, and do not condemn yourself either. Life is not about judging, but it is unjust when you err on the side of insecurity rather than seizing life with all of your efforts. Make a drawing of a pair of scales and pile on the things that make you feel good and those that make you feel awful or insecure about your self-esteem; I am certain that the side of problems will weigh more. It is your responsibility to redress the balance and adopt a very positive outlook on and approach to life. There are positive things you can do, and one of the things you must accept is that if you are not very good at something, you were either not meant to be good at it and should attempt something else, or you need more practice. When you gain familiarity with a particular task, your comfort level increases and it becomes simpler to perform.

Chapter 13: Uncertainty Regarding Males

Most likely, you are perusing this book because you lack confidence and self-esteem. You may also be wondering why males lack confidence and how they can identify their low self-esteem.

Why Do Men Lack Self-Esteem?

One of the most prevalent reasons why some males have low levels of self-confidence and self-esteem is insecurity. Simon Gelsthorpe, a clinical psychologist at the Bradford District Care NHS Foundation Trust, asserts that understanding the causes of men's confidence crises assists them in comprehending what gives them confidence.

Status, relationships, and cultural values support confidence in most cases.

The way you appear and how your body functions can have an impact on your confidence.

Even if a single factor is compromised, your physical performance and mental health can be negatively impacted. For instance, if your status changes or you lose your job, your self-esteem may decrease. If you sustain an injury, your health declines, or your body no longer functions as it once did, your self-esteem may also decrease.

Although women and men develop confidence and strength from similar sources, males are more likely to experience a confidence crisis when confronting emotional issues. Men are typically reluctant to discuss, communicate, and confront issues.

Toxic Masculinity

One of the causes of men's confidence crises is preconceived notions. Dr. Gary Wood, a social psychologist, asserts that males generally believe they must be superior to other people. They believe they must be self-reliant, independent, and strong. In fact, they believe they must be physically and mentally superior to women.

This type of belief places them under pressure, causing them to repress and reject anything deemed effeminate or feminine. They experience greater difficulty in requesting assistance for emotional problems. Men typically adhere to the "no sissy stuff" rule.

However, according to Dr. Wood, this norm is detrimental to mental health. Men are not less masculine for crying and experiencing emotional difficulties. It actually makes them healthier people.

Body Shame

In 2016, a study of over one hundred thousand males was conducted to determine how their body image affects their self-confidence. Less than half of the participants were content with their physical appearance. This dissatisfaction induces melancholy, low self-esteem, and anxiety.

Comparing yourself to others can be poisonous; therefore, you should avoid doing so. People frequently post filtered versions of themselves on social media these days. They portray themselves as flawless, making those who view their posts feel inadequate.

As much as feasible, you should avoid visiting these websites. If you visit these websites, bear in mind that you possess your own exceptional qualities. Instead of comparing yourself to others, you must concentrate on achieving your personal best. If you must compare yourself to someone, you should compare yourself to yourself.

Consider your existence six months, one year, and five years in the past. How were conditions back then? If you could compare your past self to your current self, would you be happy? If you are content with your current state, it indicates that you have improved.

Performance-Related Anxiety

Men typically have low self-esteem regarding both the appearance and functionality of their bodies. According to Dr. Wood, their masculine gender role places strain on their performance, resulting in sexual difficulties.

Sexual encounters are typically viewed as conquests and validation of masculine power. Therefore, a man with erectile dysfunction can take it personally. As a result of associating his masculinity with these issues, he may experience anxiety.

This problem is only temporary for some males. However, they should still obtain professional assistance. Additionally, many males are too proud to ask for directions. This can be a major issue.

According to researchers, men with erectile dysfunction have reduced self-esteem on average. This is due to the fact that their sexual performance and ability to sexually satisfy their companions contribute significantly to their sense of self-worth.

Actually, erectile dysfunction is quite common. In the United Kingdom, 4,3 million men have trouble maintaining or obtaining an erection. Thankfully, there is still some hope for them. Men who seek and receive treatment have an excellent chance of regaining their self-esteem, particularly if they also seek medical assistance.

How Do You Recognize Low Self-Esteem?

The majority of males are unaware that they have self-esteem issues. This is unfortunate because not recognizing a problem prevents one from pursuing solutions. If you are a male who suspects he has low self-esteem, the following indicators may serve as a wake-up call:

If You Abuse Your Spouse

A male who assaults his wife, girlfriend, or partner has a low self-esteem. He may feel compelled to demonstrate his masculinity through violence. Men who hold this view are extremely apprehensive.

Their desire to prove that they are stronger and more potent than others is overwhelming. Men with sound mental health are aware that their physical prowess should be used to protect, not injure, others.

If You Are Defined by Your Financial Situation or Lack Thereof

Many males are preoccupied with their wealth and social standing. They believe that they will be valued, admired, and esteemed when they are wealthy. They believe that prosperity places them at the pinnacle of society.

In contrast, they believe they are meaningless if they lose their money. They are always defined by their financial status. This way of thinking is harmful and toxic.

Remember that money does not define you. There is more to manhood than financial success. Therefore, you should not feel the need to flaunt your wealth and possessions so that others will consider you seriously. Even if you lack significant affluence, you should not feel devalued or inferior.

If You Are Dependent on Porn

If you frequently watch pornographic videos or read pornographic magazines, there is a high possibility that you have low self-esteem. It is even more likely if you would rather watch porn than pursue a genuine relationship with someone else.

Individuals with low self-esteem typically dread interpersonal relationships. Their low self-esteem inhibits their ability to interact and socialize with others.

Instead of seeking out a romantic partner, men with low self-esteem typically choose to satiate themselves by viewing porn. Therefore, it is time to evaluate yourself if you are always looking at porn and never venturing out.

If You Are Aggressive,

In school, students who bully their peers are more likely to have problems at home. Instead of addressing these problems, they take out their frustrations on others.

Unfortunately, maturation does not always eliminate this type of situation. Men with low self-esteem suppress their emotions and belittle others in order to feel better about themselves. They feel superior when others suffer as a result of their actions.

Never tread on other individuals. Do not intentionally harm others for your own satisfaction. A true man never intentionally harms others. Seek professional assistance or counseling if you harass your peers frequently.

If You Are Intimidated by Progressive Women,

In the past, males typically worked while women remained at home. However, things have changed today. Regarding gender equality, advances have been made. Increasing numbers of women are assuming roles that were formerly reserved for males.

Today, there are numerous accomplished women in numerous industries. They are intelligent, affluent, assertive, and assured. Men with robust self-esteem do not perceive these women as a threat. In fact, they recognize and appreciate their value.

Conversely, males with low self-esteem experience insecurity. This hinders their ability to engage, date, and interact with these women. Even worse, they may attempt to bring them down so they can regain their sense of control.

If You Escaping Responsibility

Men who are genuinely manly face their responsibilities without fear. Even if they are afraid or perplexed, they still carry out their responsibilities. They are aware that others are relying on them and do not wish to let anyone down.

Men with low self-esteem, on the other hand, cannot manage the responsibility. They flee whenever things become difficult. They are afraid of accumulating expectations and failure.

For instance, some males flee when they impregnate a woman. Real males, however, remain and accept their responsibilities. Some men, including their children, forsake their families due to financial difficulties. Men of character choose to discover a solution.

If You Hold Others Responsible

Men with low self-esteem are unable to embrace their flaws. They place the responsibility for their errors on others. They believe that making an error diminishes their masculinity. Thus, they never aim the finger in their own direction. They are unaware of the significance of an apology.

If You Make Others Have Sexual Contact

Mature and self-assured males do not need to use force to have sex with a woman. They are confident in their ability to captivate women and win their favor.

In extreme circumstances, men with extremely low self-esteem resort to rape. These individuals are not in a proper state of mind. Do not delay until you reach this point. If you find yourself having thoughts of rape, consult a mental health professional for assistance.

If You Are Overly Guarded

Men with healthy self-esteem do not sense the need to exert control over their partner. They are not envious without sufficient cause. They do not restrict their partner's ability to make acquaintances and have a social life. They are not insecure and fearful that their companion will abandon them for another person. Men with confidence know that they are worthy of their partner's affection and respect.

You must reevaluate yourself if you find yourself harboring negative thoughts about your companion, such as suspicions that she is flirting with or talking to someone else. Consider why you are having these thoughts. Could you be experiencing insecurity? If so, you must remind yourself of your positive attributes. Consult a therapist if necessary.

If You Desire Your Ex's Failure or Discontentment

After a breakup or divorce, mentally and emotionally healthy individuals are able to move on. They are confident that they will meet someone new or who is a better match for them. They do not rush into a relationship because they can exist independently. They are content when they are alone.

Those with low self-esteem, on the other hand, cannot function without a partner. They are overly reliant on their partner for finances, housework, and emotional support. They are helpless without a companion to accompany them. They lack confidence in their ability to accomplish tasks on their own.

Therefore, when their companion abandons them, these individuals become bitter and resentful. They become unreasonable and furious. They wish to exact revenge on their ex. They wish their ex-partner ill fortune for abandoning them and no longer meeting their requirements.

Try to recall your most recent romantic relationship. Why did it terminate, and what did you do following its conclusion? Did you wallow in sorrow and attempt to gain back your ex? Or did you attempt to move on by concentrating on your health and finding joy in other things?

If you still experience anger or bitterness toward your ex, you are not in a healthy mental state. You can only claim to have moved on when you are apathetic or sincerely pleased for your ex.

If You Are a Persecutor

Men who lack self-assurance and self-belief solely admire women from a distance. They lack the self-assurance to approach and introduce themselves. They engage in online and offline surveillance.

They may, for instance, seek for the woman's social media profile or follow her through the mall. This type of conduct is actually disturbing and can lead to trouble. Therefore, instead of being a stalker, you must muster the courage to introduce yourself in an appropriate manner.

If You Settle for Less

Men with low self-esteem maintain dysfunctional and unhealthy relationships. They do not believe they can find someone who will love and care for them more. They believe they cannot survive without their companion. They do not believe they deserve to be cherished and cared for.

These males typically pursue emotionally unavailable, married, mentally unstable, violent, or addicted women. They remain in unhealthy relationships because they lack the confidence to initiate and maintain healthy relationships.

Consider your past relationships and reassess them. Were they wholesome?

Were they advantageous to your health? What were the benefits of these relationships? If your previous relationships did not aid in your personal growth and development, you may need to reconsider the types of relationships you have.

If You Have Alcoholism

If the only time you feel alive is when you consume excessive amounts of alcohol, you may lack confidence. If you abuse alcohol, you will feel depressed and exhausted when abstaining. You will become estranged and disconnected from reality.

If You Are Unfaithful or a Cheater, You Must Repent

Cheaters are more often than not mentally and emotionally disturbed.

They deceive because they lack sufficient self-esteem and self-confidence to consider themselves deserving of a healthy relationship.

Men with a high sense of self-worth are cheerful and content in their relationships. They do not sense the need to bolster their ego through womanizing and infidelity. They protect their relationship because they value it.

If You Suffer Peer Pressure

People who are readily influenced by others typically lack sufficient self-confidence. They frequently yield to peer pressure in an effort to be liked and accepted.

Children and adolescents are the most frequent victims of peer pressure. However, with sufficient guidance, they eventually mature and progress. You should have already surmounted peer pressure as an adult male. If not, you should exercise caution in your actions and decisions. You should consult a counselor or mental health professional if necessary.

Chapter 14: The Components Of Self-Esteem.

This section describes confidence and outlines extant perspectives on the topic. Confidence is a sociometer, essentially an internal indicator of how esteemed or devalued one is as a social partner.

The section evaluates a progression of explicit, testable hypotheses about confidence and other discoveries pertinent to the sociometer hypothesis and its particular theories. In unambiguous terms, individual confidence refers to a person's assessment of their own worth and how they feel about their abilities and limitations. Global confidence refers to a global evaluation of one's value, whereas region-specific confidence involves examinations of one's worth in a particular region. Self-confidence is an emotionally charged evaluation.

Self-evaluations are evaluations of one's behavior or credits along evaluative dimensions; however, few self-evaluations are objective. whereas others are emotionally charged.

Individual differences in dispositional or characteristic confidence are the foundation of confidence. When you have solid confidence, you feel much better about yourself and believe you deserve others' admiration. When you have low self-esteem, you place little value on your thoughts and opinions. Trust in one's value as a person is a valuable mental asset and, in general, a deeply certain figure in life; it has been correlated with success, significant relationships, and fulfillment.

A lack of self-respect can lead to discouragement, underestimation of one's true capacity, and exposure to detrimental relationships and circumstances.

Regard for oneself is comprised of four components: self-esteem, identity, a sense of belonging, and competence.

Self-assurance (a sense of safety).

This is the foundation of assurance. Assuming that we have a sense of security within our family, that we are cherished, and that our needs are met, we develop confidence.

This is the point at which we attempt to establish ourselves and initiate new endeavors and experiences.

Again, as an illustration, when figuring out how to walk, we frequently fall down the underlying surface, but with encouragement, we cultivate our conviction and effort!

Identity.

This is the knowledge we have of ourselves; through testing, learning, and receiving feedback from those around us, we come to understand our attributes, capacities, needs, and emotions. The personality can be divided into several sections: physical (the depiction that

every individual has of their own body) and social (how I interact with others, the groups I associate with, my financial situation, my position as an understudy, laborer, or high school student, how I act with my partner or partner, etc.).

Feeling of belonging.

We all have a place with various groups, including family, friends, education, and sports teams.

We likewise characterize ourselves by belonging to these gatherings, by the connections we have with others, and by the experiences we have in these gatherings: feeling like a part of a gathering, feeling fortitude, searching out the other gathering individuals, communicating well, sharing, etc. The various groups we belong to allow us to feel understood and recognize that there are others who are similar to us.

A sense of competence.

To feel capable, we seek a variety of experiences, successes and failures, and new knowledge. The sensation of skill is related to inspiration: a person is motivated when confronted with challenges that they can overcome.

Achievement generates a sense of viability and pride that boosts confidence and encourages the individual to accept new challenges; however, confidence is not set in stone. It shifts and settles in brightness

of the people we meet and our own heritage. Even though immaturity tends to be a test, one thing is certain: the more circumstances we encounter, the more we learn about ourselves and the better we understand our identity, who we need to relate to, what we would rather not revisit, and what we require for our lives.

www.ingramcontent.com/pod-product-compliance
Lightning Source LLC
Chambersburg PA
CBHW050250120526
44590CB00016B/2293